D1110832

HELLO AND WELCOME

GOING ON A ROAD TRIP CAN BE GREAT FUN AND EXCITING, IN THIS ROAD TRIP ACTIVITY BOOK YOU WILL BE ABLE TO DRAW, FIND, SOLVE AND SEARCH MANY ROAD TRIP THEMED ACTIVITIES INCLUDING UNIQUE HAND DRAWN MAZES- CHECK OUT OUR BACK PAGE FOR EXAMPLES

GRAB A PEN OR PENCIL AND BE EXCITED TO COMPLETE THIS ACTIVITY BOOK.

ACTIVITIES INCLUDE
- STORY MAZES
- ROAD SIGN BINGO
- WORD GAMES
- WORD SEARCH
- SUDOKU
- BRAIN TEASER PROBLEMS
- CROSSWORDS
- AND MORE

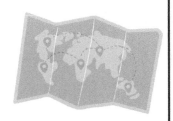

PEOPLE SPOTTING
TRY AND SPOT THESE PEOPLE ALONG THE WAY
PUT A X ON TO THE ONES YOU SEE

PERSON ON THE PHONE	SOMEONE WEARING SUNGLASSES	SOMEONE RIDING A BIKE
FARMER ON TRACTOR	CHEF	SOMEONE SLEEPING
A BABY	POLICE OFFICER	SOMEONE WITH A PET
SOMEONE WALKING A DOG	HITCHHIKER	CONSTRUCTION WORKER
SOMEONE JOGGING	A FAMIILY	A SECURITY GUARD

ASK FELLOW PASSENGERS TO HELP

MATCH THE TRAVEL ICONS

UNSCRAMBLE THESE WORDS 1

LETTER HINT IS PROVIDED

OPST

S _ _ _

OOFD

F _ _ _

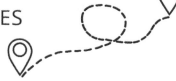

NGSI

_ _ G _

ETTRES

S _ _ _ _ _

ESPLE

_ _ _ _ P

YSKE

K _ _ _

HAMBURGER VS FRIES

WHAT IS THERE MORE OF

YOU'RE GOING AWAY ON HOLIDAY

GUIDE THE PLANE TO THE AIRPORT

ROAD SIGN SEARCH
TRY AND SPOT THESE ROAD SIGNS
PUT A X ON TO THE ONES YOU SEE

ASK FELLOW PASSENGERS TO HELP

UNSCRAMBLE THESE WORDS 3

LETTER HINT IS PROVIDED

CTRKU — T _ U _ K

LHLI — H _ L _

WREYEFA — F _ E E _ _ _

IYDAOLH — H _ _ _ _ _ Y

TMLEO — M O _ _ _

TESICSAU — S U _ _ _ _ _ E

CVOAINTA — V _ C _ _ _ _ N

ANIMAL SAFARI SEARCH
TRY AND SPOT THESE ANIMALS ON YOUR TRIP
PUT A X ON TO THE ONES YOU SEE

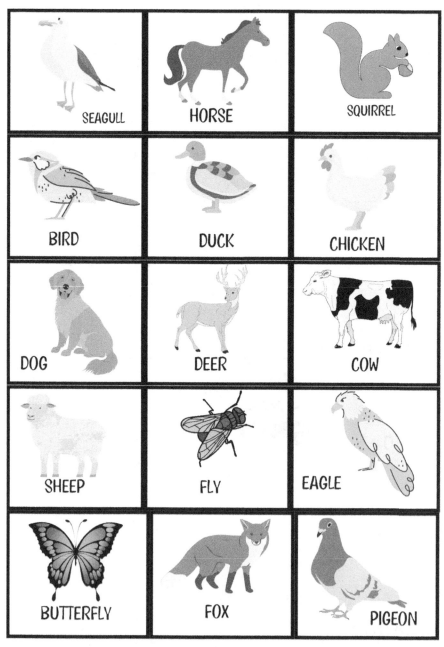

ASK FELLOW PASSENGERS TO JOIN IN

CAN YOU COMPLETE THE PLANE DRAWING

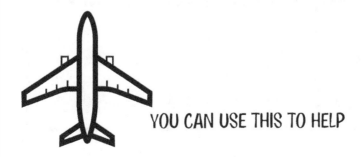

YOU CAN USE THIS TO HELP

CAN YOU SEE THESE SIGNS

TRY AND SPOT THESE SIGNS ALONG THE WAY
PUT A X ON TO THE ONES YOU SEE

CAN YOU GET TO THE HOLIDAY HOUSE

COMPLETE THE MAZE

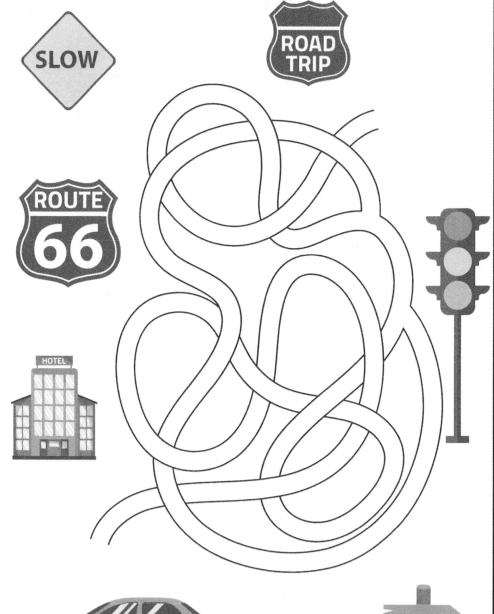

CAN YOU GET TO THE WAY IN

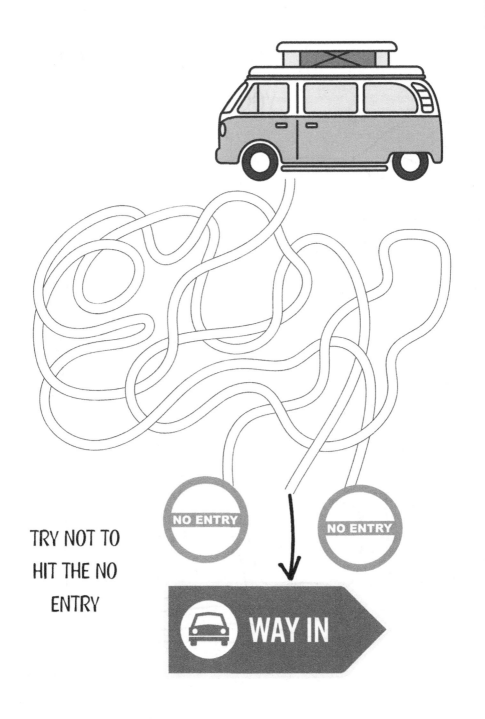

TRY NOT TO HIT THE NO ENTRY

NO ENTRY

NO ENTRY

WAY IN

PICK UP ALL THE ITEMS/HITCHHIKER BEFORE YOU GET TO THE HIGHWAY

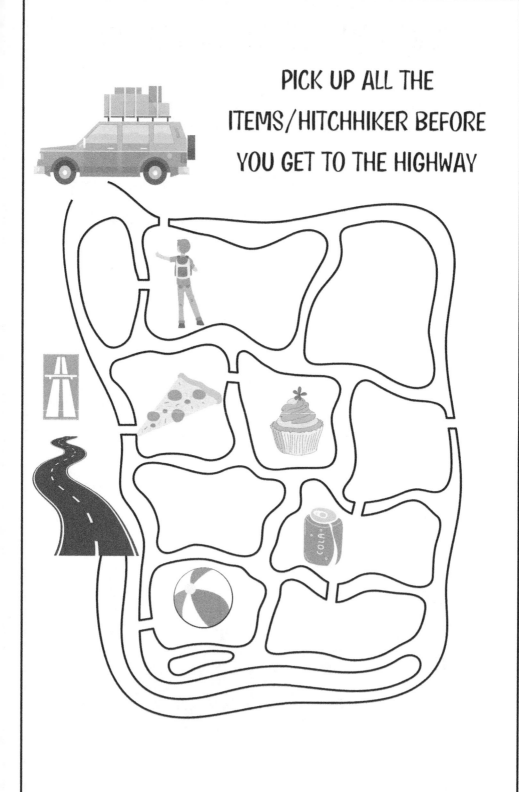

COMPLETE THE MAZE

TIME FOR THE BEACH

CAN YOU GUIDE THE CAR
TO THE BEACH

EVERYBODY IS HUNGRY

USE THE MAP AND GET TO THE FOOD

UNSCRAMBLE THESE WORDS 2

LETTER HINT IS PROVIDED

ANEL   L _ _ _

EARVTL   T _ _ _ _ L

IREDRV   D _ I _ _ _

TRES   R _ _ _ _

ASFT   _ _ S _

AIRN   R _ _ _

OUERT   R _ U _ _

CAN YOU FIND THE WORDS

ASK FRIENDS OR FAMILY TO JOIN IN

R	E	A	R	T	H	U	G
Y	S	A	E	C	R	U	R
D	E	E	P	T	I	N	Y
N	I	K	L	R	I	A	F
M	A	G	I	L	E	M	Z
T	I	Y	Z	Z	U	F	E
U	A	D	A	P	T	D	M
Z	L	P	B	R	A	S	H

ADAPT   AGILE

BRASH   DEEP

DIM   DULL

EARTH   EASY

ECRU   EMIT

FAIR   FUZZY

KIN   REAR

TINY

CAN YOU FIND THE WORDS

ASK FRIENDS OR FAMILY TO JOIN IN

Z	H	Y	P	P	A	H	J
D	U	S	T	Y	O	Q	U
Z	S	Y	A	M	C	G	I
D	E	V	O	L	R	I	C
N	D	L	I	H	C	I	Y
E	A	B	E	I	G	E	F
W	N	D	Y	G	G	O	F
B	I	R	C	M	I	L	E

BEIGE

CLASH

DUSTY

FOGGY

ICY

LOVED

NEW

CHILD

CRIB

FIRM

HAPPY

JUICY

MILE

SEDAN

COMPLETE THE WORD SEARCH

ASK FRIENDS OR FAMILY TO JOIN IN

E	C	A	T	E	R	M	L
N	U	A	S	I	A	G	V
X	U	L	L	U	H	U	E
F	R	F	B	M	R	S	F
U	L	L	O	O	C	C	R
N	F	O	R	M	L	S	E
N	D	O	T	E	Z	D	S
Y	P	K	C	O	Z	Y	H

ASIA   BLUE

BOLD   CALM

CATER   COOL

COZY   ROAD TRIP   DOTE

ECRU   FORM

FRESH   FUN

FUNNY   HUE

HOW QUICK CAN YOU FIND THESE

ASK FRIENDS OR FAMILY TO JOIN IN

```
T   O   T   R   E   L   A   G
U   W   O   D   M   A   R   S
M   S   Y   F   L   A   S   H
B   A   S   C   H   I   L   D
E   L   E   F   L   U   U   R
I   T   A   R   I   O   E   B
G   Y   F   R   C   R   U   G
E   N   A   G   E   V   M   D
```

ALERT	BEIGE
BLARE	BUILD
CHILD	CREAM
FIRM	FLASH
HUE	LOUD
MARS	SALTY
TOT	TOYS
VEGAN	

CAN YOU FIND THE WORDS

ASK FRIENDS OR FAMILY TO JOIN IN

```
W  C  J  E  V  I  R  D
P  N  O  A  S  H  Y  Z
F  E  C  L  M  D  Z  T
L  H  V  A  O  M  I  A
O  F  A  I  R  R  Y  K
W  I  V  B  L  E  N  D
D  I  R  T  Y  A  L  P
Y  D  D  E  C  I  D  Q
```

ALIVE	ASHY
BLEND	CARE
COLOR	DICED
DIRTY	DRIVE
FAIR	FLOW
JAMMY	KID

COMPLETE THE WORD SEARCH

ASK FRIENDS OR FAMILY TO JOIN IN

T	E	T	D	N	B	A	F
H	R	Z	R	L	A	D	R
E	A	O	A	E	O	L	N
B	V	L	L	L	L	B	C
B	I	I	O	O	B	A	A
A	J	R	L	O	C	K	M
R	O	C	C	A	R	E	E
E	Y	C	H	I	L	D	L

ALERT   ALIVE

BAKED   BARE

BLAZE   BOLD

CAMEL      CHILD

CLAN   COLOR

CRIB   DROOL

JOY

HOW QUICK CAN YOU FIND THESE

ASK FRIENDS OR FAMILY TO JOIN IN

S	M	H	C	R	A	M	F
L	S	J	R	U	H	I	A
S	A	I	B	A	R	L	D
D	E	I	K	L	E	E	E
I	E	P	S	B	O	L	D
R	N	P	U	A	E	N	C
T	H	A	T	O	W	E	D
Y	Z	T	W	H	C	I	W

ASIA	BLOND
BOLD	CLEAR
COUPE	CURED
DEPTH	DIRTY
FADED	KISS
MARCH	MILE
WAN	WEE

CAN YOU FILL IN THE WORDS

ASK A GROWN UP TO HELP IF YOU ARE STUCK

GAME 1

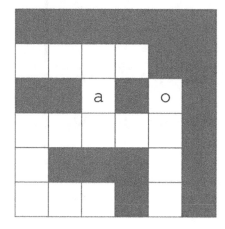

THERE ARE HINTS IN THE GRID

GAME 2

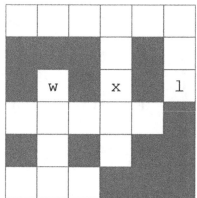

skyed

may

same

odes

sip

pot

coded

woks

mixes

ash

thymus

sol

STILL FINDING IT TRICKY? ANSWERS ARE ON THE BACK PAGES

CAN YOU FILL IN THE WORDS

ASK A GROWN UP TO HELP IF YOU ARE STUCK

GAME 3

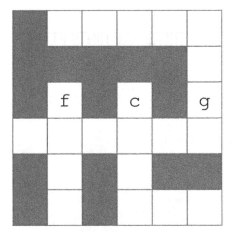

THERE ARE HINTS IN THE GRID

GAME 4

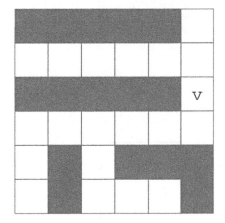

tights
hags
cough
file
chum
mys

archly
levy
riddle
cud
dos
aid

STILL FINDING IT TRICKY? ANSWERS ARE ON THE BACK PAGES

ANSWERS ON THE BACK PAGE

CAN YOU FILL IN THE WORDS

ASK A GROWN UP TO HELP IF YOU ARE STUCK

GAME 5

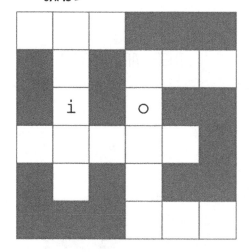

THERE ARE HINTS IN THE GRID

GAME 6

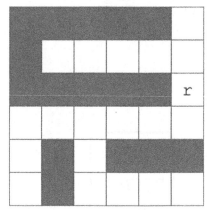

slows
rowed
tails
nth
duh
roe

sobbed
bird
alibi
big
sir
garb

STILL FINDING IT TRICKY? ANSWERS ARE ON THE BACK PAGES

SYMBOL MATHS

EACH SHAPE HAS A NUMERIC VALUE, BUT IT IS UNKNOWN.
WORKING OUT THE EQUATIONS HELPS TO FIGURE OUT THE VALUES OF THE SHAPES.

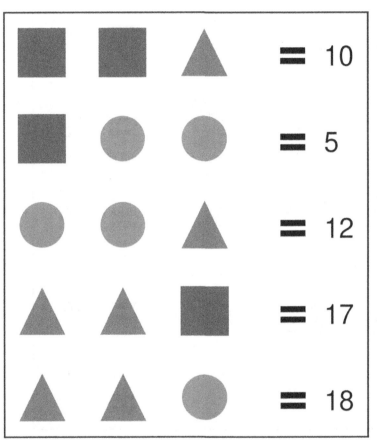

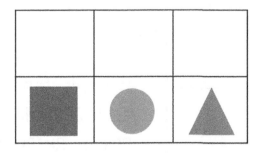

HINT: THE EQUATIONS ARE ADDITION, IN EACH ROW THE SHAPES ARE ADDED TOGETHER.

SYMBOL MATHS

EACH SHAPE HAS A NUMERIC VALUE, BUT IT IS UNKNOWN.
WORKING OUT THE EQUATIONS HELPS TO FIGURE OUT THE VALUES OF THE
SHAPES.

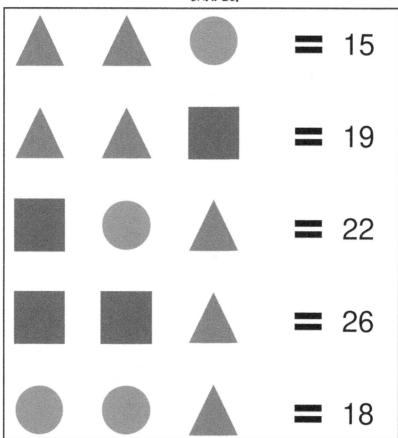

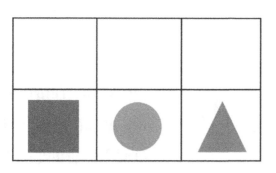

HINT: THE EQUATIONS
ARE ADDITION, IN EACH
ROW THE SHAPES ARE
ADDED TOGETHER.

ANSWER 2

CAN YOU COMPLETE THE BIKE DRAWING

YOU CAN USE THIS TO HELP

SYMBOL MATHS

EACH SHAPE HAS A NUMERIC VALUE, BUT IT IS UNKNOWN.
WORKING OUT THE EQUATIONS HELPS TO FIGURE OUT THE VALUES OF THE
SHAPES.

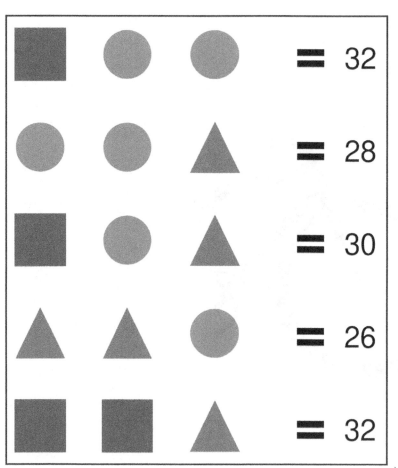

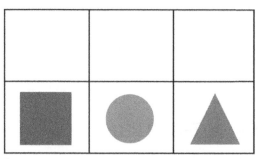

ANSWER 3

HINT: THE EQUATIONS
ARE ADDITION, IN EACH
ROW THE SHAPES ARE
ADDED TOGETHER.

SYMBOL MATHS

EACH SHAPE HAS A NUMERIC VALUE, BUT IT IS UNKNOWN.
WORKING OUT THE EQUATIONS HELPS TO FIGURE OUT THE VALUES OF THE
SHAPES.

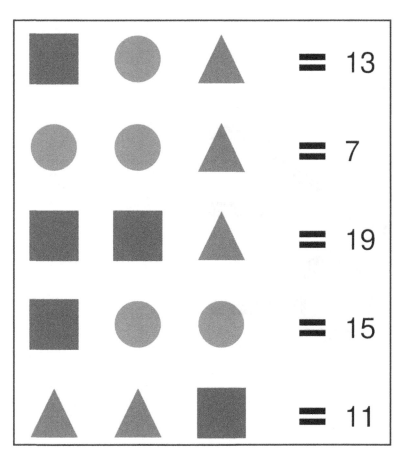

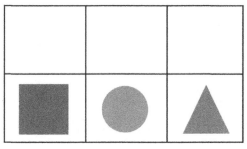

HINT: THE EQUATIONS
ARE ADDITION, IN EACH
ROW THE SHAPES ARE
ADDED TOGETHER.

ANSWER 4

CAN YOU COMPLETE THE CAR DRAWING

YOU CAN USE THIS TO HELP

SYMBOL MATHS

EACH SHAPE HAS A NUMERIC VALUE, BUT IT IS UNKNOWN.
WORKING OUT THE EQUATIONS HELPS TO FIGURE OUT THE VALUES OF THE
SHAPES.

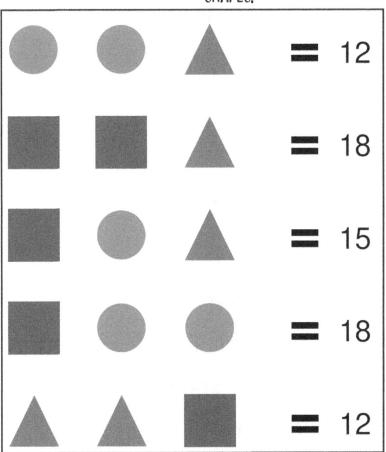

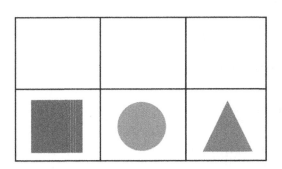

HINT: THE EQUATIONS
ARE ADDITION, IN EACH
ROW THE SHAPES ARE
ADDED TOGETHER.

DURING YOUR TRIP WHICH OF THESE HAVE YOU SEEN OR DONE

TRY A NEW FOOD ☐

RIDE A GO CART ☐

TAKE A SELFIE ☐

RIDE A HORSE ☐

SWIM IN A LAKE ☐

SEE A SUNSET ☐

TOUR A CAVE ☐

SEE A SUNRISE ☐

BUILD A SAND CASTLE ☐

STOP AT A PETROL STATION ☐

HAVE A HOT DRINK ☐

MAKE A NEW FRIEND ☐

SEE WILD ANIMALS ☐

ASK FOR DIRECTIONS ☐

SEE A WATERFALL ☐

PET A FARM ANIMAL ☐

MATCHING FUN

MATCH THESE BELOW

GAME 1

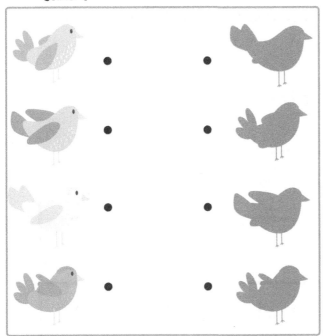

GAME 2

SUDOKU GAME 1

HOW QUICK CAN YOU COMPLETE THE PUZZLE

 COMPLETED IN ·

6	3	2	5	1	4
	1		6		
1		4	2		5
	2	6	4		
				6	2

 A COMPLETED PUZZLE HAS THE NUMBERS 1-6 IN EACH
ROW, IN EACH COLUMN,
AND IN EACH INNER BOX.
TO START, SOME NUMBERS ARE REMOVED.
SOLVING THE PUZZLE MEANS FIGURING OUT WHAT THE
NUMBERS TO FILL BACK IN.

SUDOKU GAME 2

HOW QUICK CAN YOU COMPLETE THE PUZZLE

 COMPLETED IN ....

3		6	2	4	
	2	5		6	
2		3	5		4
			6	3	
6	4	2	3		1
5					6

SUDOKU GAME 3

HOW QUICK CAN YOU COMPLETE THE PUZZLE

 COMPLETED IN ....

			5	1	3
3	1				
5	3			2	6
		1	3	4	5
	4		2	5	
1			6		

SUDOKU GAME 4

HOW QUICK CAN YOU COMPLETE THE PUZZLE

COMPLETED IN . . . .

1			2		
		5		6	
	3	6			2
2	5	1		4	
	1		6	2	4
6	4	2	1		

SUDOKU GAME 5

HOW QUICK CAN YOU COMPLETE THE PUZZLE

 COMPLETED IN ....

3	4	1	5	6	
	5		4	3	1
		2	6		
4			2	1	3
	1			2	5
5	2				6

WILD ANIMAL CROSSWORD
ASK A GROWN UP TO HELP

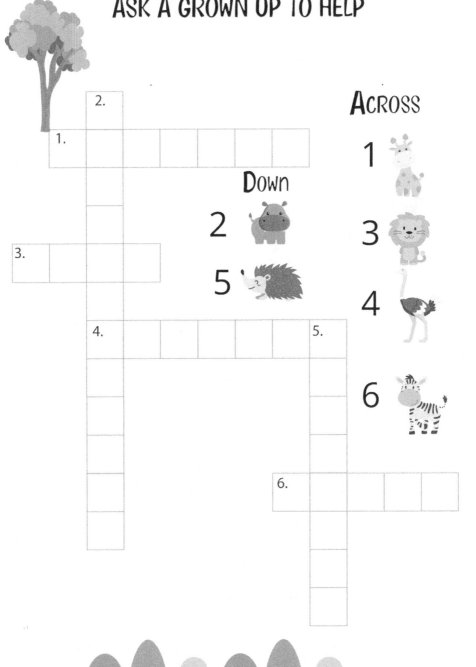

Across

1

3

4

6

Down

2

5

ROAD TRIP CROSS WORD

ASK A GROWN UP TO HELP

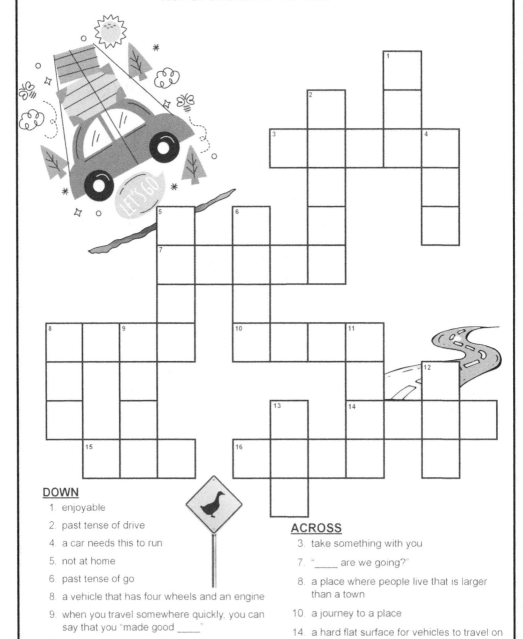

DOWN

1. enjoyable
2. past tense of drive
4. a car needs this to run
5. not at home
6. past tense of go
8. a vehicle that has four wheels and an engine
9. when you travel somewhere quickly, you can say that you "made good ____"
11. to leave a car in a particular place
12. a vehicle that is larger than a car
13. a picture showing the roads of an area

ACROSS

3. take something with you
7. "____ are we going?"
8. a place where people live that is larger than a town
10. a journey to a place
14. a hard flat surface for vehicles to travel on
15. Kids often ask: "Are we there ____?"
16. to put things into a bag to take with you

COMPLETE THE MAZE

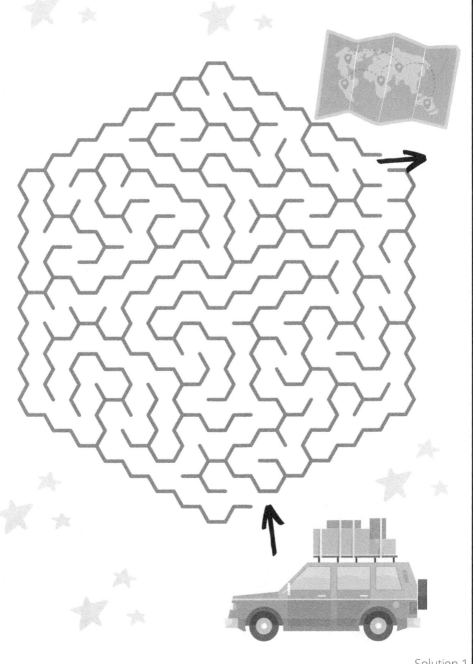

COMPLETE THE MAZE
GET TO THE MIDDLE

COMPLETE THE MAZE

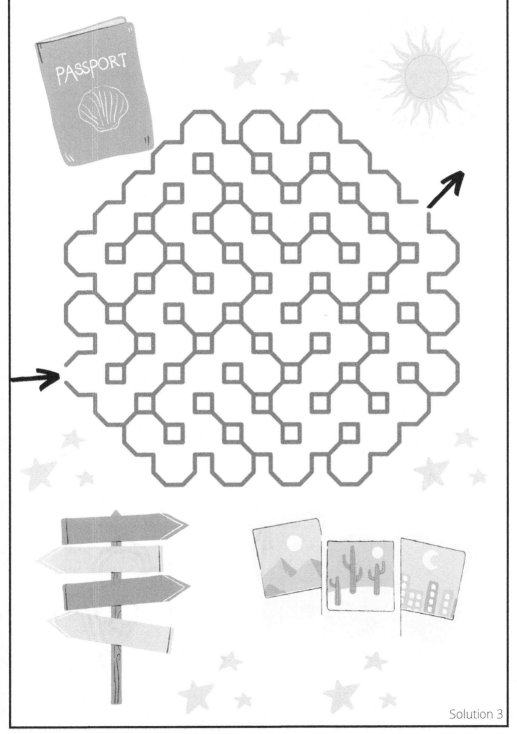

COMPLETE THE MAZE

COMPLETE THE MAZE

COMPLETE THE MAZE

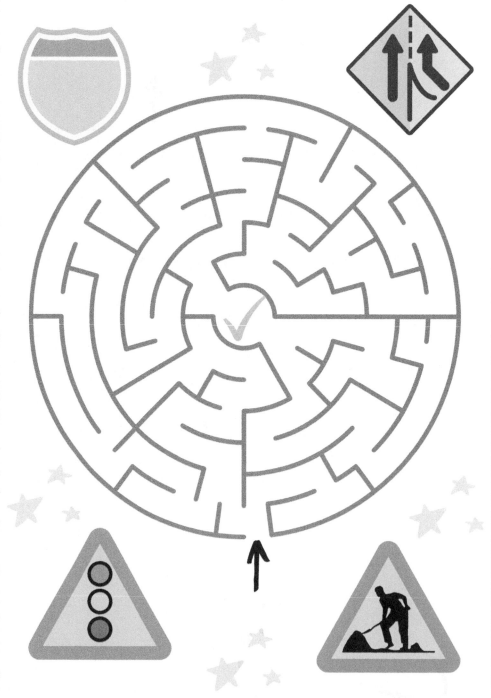

Solution 6

COMPLETE THE MAZE

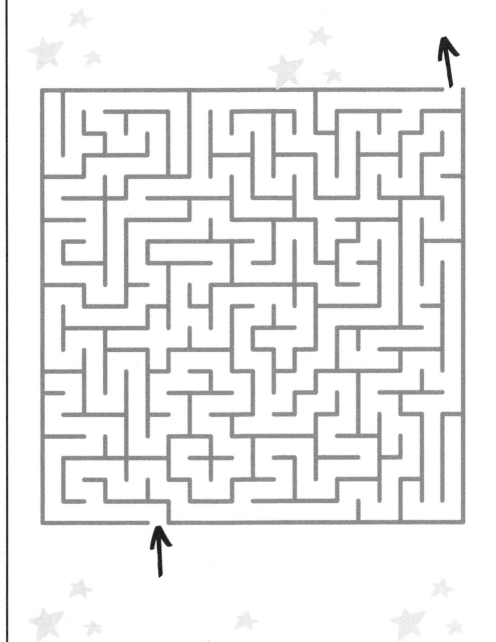

MAGIC SQUARES

SOLVE THE PUZZLES

EVERY, ROW, COLUMN AND DIAGONAL MUST ADD UP TO **15**

FILL IN THE GAPS

	7	6
9	5	1
4		8

FILL IN THE GAPS

9	3		16	15
2	21	20		8
25	19	13	7	
18	12	6	5	24
		4	23	17

EVERY, ROW, COLUMN AND DIAGONAL MUST ADD UP TO **65**

ADDITION FUN

1)   98
    +   14
    ‾‾‾‾‾‾‾‾

2)   12
    +   14
    ‾‾‾‾‾‾‾‾

3)   24
    +   33
    ‾‾‾‾‾‾‾‾

4)   98
    +   50
    ‾‾‾‾‾‾‾‾

5)   89
    +   89
    ‾‾‾‾‾‾‾‾

6)   76
    +   28
    ‾‾‾‾‾‾‾‾

7)   83
    +   91
    ‾‾‾‾‾‾‾‾

8)   13
    +   82
    ‾‾‾‾‾‾‾‾

9)   74
    +   82
    ‾‾‾‾‾‾‾‾

10)   63
    +   72
    ‾‾‾‾‾‾‾‾

11)   69
    +   89
    ‾‾‾‾‾‾‾‾

12)   13
    +   37
    ‾‾‾‾‾‾‾‾

13)   42
    +   63
    ‾‾‾‾‾‾‾‾

14)   57
    +   90
    ‾‾‾‾‾‾‾‾

15)   79
    +   19
    ‾‾‾‾‾‾‾‾

SUBTRACTION
FUN

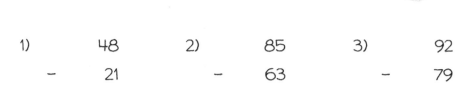

1)   48
  −   21
_____

2)   85
  −   63
_____

3)   92
  −   79
_____

4)   63
  −   13
_____

5)   56
  −   14
_____

6)   69
  −   11
_____

7)   75
  −   14
_____

8)   43
  −   21
_____

9)   86
  −   18
_____

10)   82
  −   71
_____

11)   68
  −   64
_____

12)   47
  −   26
_____

13)   80
  −   46
_____

14)   56
  −   36
_____

15)   51
  −   41
_____

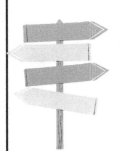

MULTIPLICATION
FUN

1)   1
  x   9
_____

2)   8
  x   3
_____

3)   1
  x   3
_____

4)   4
  x   9
_____

5)   5
  x   5
_____

6)   2
  x   6
_____

7)   4
  x   1
_____

8)   5
  x   9
_____

9)   6
  x   7
_____

10)   1
  x   2
_____

11)   2
  x   7
_____

12)   1
  x   6
_____

13)   5
  x   7
_____

14)   7
  x   2
_____

15)   3
  x   4
_____

ADDITION AND SUBTRACTION FUN

1)
$$\begin{array}{r} 92 \\ +\ 16 \\ \hline \end{array}$$

2)
$$\begin{array}{r} 81 \\ +\ 59 \\ \hline \end{array}$$

3)
$$\begin{array}{r} 55 \\ +\ 42 \\ \hline \end{array}$$

4)
$$\begin{array}{r} 30 \\ -\ 15 \\ \hline \end{array}$$

5)
$$\begin{array}{r} 51 \\ -\ 41 \\ \hline \end{array}$$

6)
$$\begin{array}{r} 56 \\ +\ 37 \\ \hline \end{array}$$

7)
$$\begin{array}{r} 91 \\ -\ 34 \\ \hline \end{array}$$

8)
$$\begin{array}{r} 85 \\ -\ 71 \\ \hline \end{array}$$

9)
$$\begin{array}{r} 67 \\ -\ 53 \\ \hline \end{array}$$

10)
$$\begin{array}{r} 60 \\ -\ 60 \\ \hline \end{array}$$

11)
$$\begin{array}{r} 56 \\ -\ 40 \\ \hline \end{array}$$

12)
$$\begin{array}{r} 71 \\ +\ 11 \\ \hline \end{array}$$

13)
$$\begin{array}{r} 72 \\ +\ 58 \\ \hline \end{array}$$

14)
$$\begin{array}{r} 40 \\ -\ 31 \\ \hline \end{array}$$

15)
$$\begin{array}{r} 73 \\ +\ 32 \\ \hline \end{array}$$

TIC TAC TOE FUN

YOU DONT HAVE TO CHOOSE Xs OR Os

Winner ....

TIC TAC TOE FUN

YOU DONT HAVE TO CHOOSE Xs OR Os

Winner ....

TIC TAC TOE FUN

YOU DONT HAVE TO CHOOSE Xs OR Os

Winner ....

TIC TAC TOE FUN

You dont have to choose Xs or Os

Winner . . . .

TIC TAC TOE FUN

You dont have to choose Xs or Os

Winner ....

DOTS AND BOXES GAME

PLAYERS TAKE TURNS IN DRAWING LINES BETWEEN DOTS ON A GRID. THE PLAYER WHO COMPLETES THE MOST BOXES WINS. IF A PLAYER COMPLETES THE FOURTH SIDE OF A BOX THEY INITIAL THAT BOX AND MUST DRAW ANOTHER LINE.

GAME 1

GAME 2

Winner ....

DOTS AND BOXES GAME

GAME 1

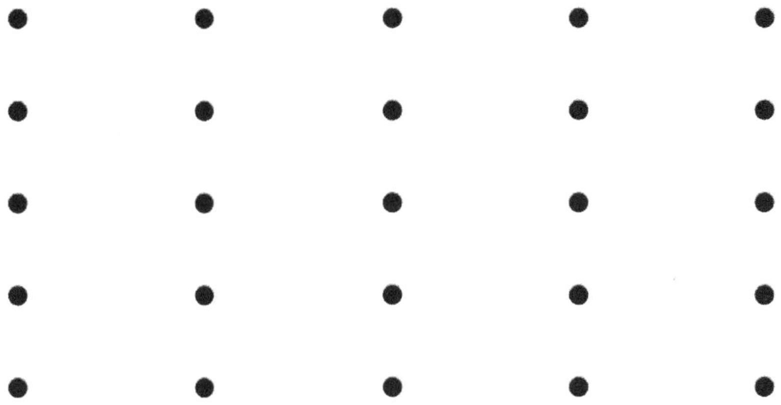

· · · · ·

· · · · ·

· · · · ·

· · · · ·

· · · · ·

GAME 2

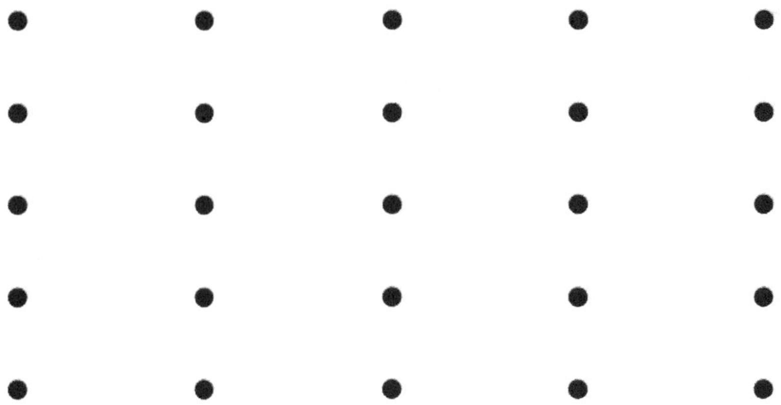

· · · · ·

· · · · ·

· · · · ·

· · · · ·

· · · · ·

Winner ....

DOTS AND BOXES GAME

GAME 1

GAME 2

Winner ....

DOTS AND BOXES GAME

GAME 1

GAME 2

Winner ....

POCKET HANGMAN

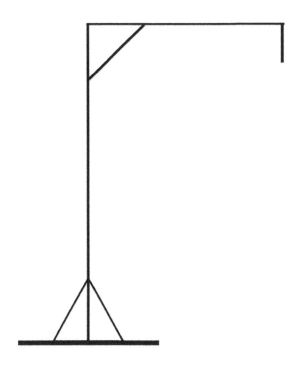

_ _ _ _ _ _ _ _ _ _ _ _ _

_ _ _ _ _ _ _ _ _ _ _ _ _

A B C D E F G H I J K L M

N O P Q R S T U V W X Y Z

Winner ....

POCKET HANGMAN

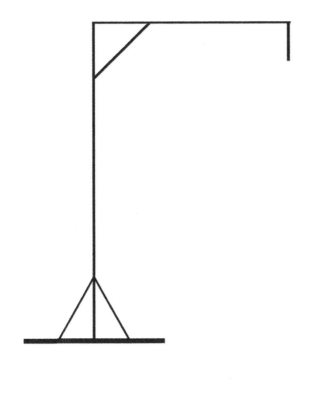

_ _ _ _ _ _ _ _ _ _ _ _ _ _ _ _ _ _ _

_ _ _ _ _ _ _ _ _ _ _ _ _ _ _ _ _ _ _

A B C D E F G H I J K L M

N O P Q R S T U V W X Y Z

Winner ....

POCKET HANGMAN

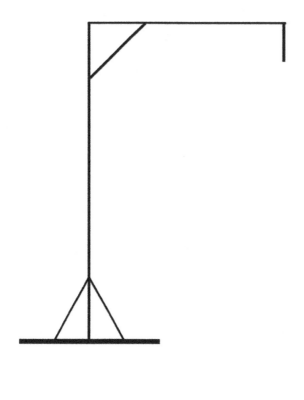

_ _ _ _ _ _ _ _ _ _ _ _ _ _ _

_ _ _ _ _ _ _ _ _ _ _ _ _ _ _

A B C D E F G H I J K L M

N O P Q R S T U V W X Y Z

Winner ....

POCKET HANGMAN

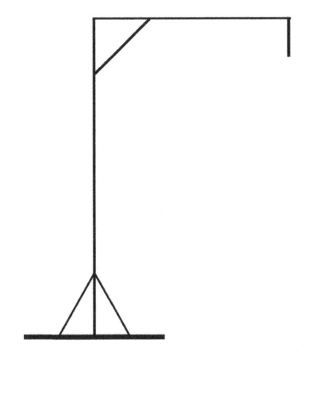

_ _ _ _ _ _ _ _ _ _ _ _ _ _ _

_ _ _ _ _ _ _ _ _ _ _ _ _ _ _

A B C D E F G H I J K L M

N O P Q R S T U V W X Y Z

Winner ....

POCKET HANGMAN

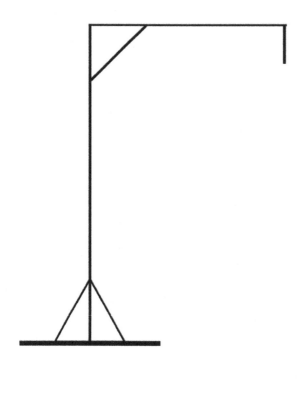

_ _ _ _ _ _ _ _ _ _ _ _ _ _ _ _

_ _ _ _ _ _ _ _ _ _ _ _ _ _ _ _

A B C D E F G H I J K L M

N O P Q R S T U V W X Y Z

Winner ....

SOLUTIONS

IF YOU NEED THEM

OPST	STOP
OOFD	FOOD
NGSI	SIGN
ETTRES	STREET
ESPLE	SLEEP
YSKE	KEYS

UNSCRAMBLE
ANSWERS 1

ANEL	LANE
EARVTL	TRAVEL
IREDRV	DRIVER
TRES	REST
ASFT	FAST
AIRN	RAIN
OUERT	ROUTE

UNSCRAMBLE
ANSWERS 2

CTRKU	TRUCK
LHLI	HILL
WREYEFA	FREEWAY
IYDAOLH	HOLIDAY
TMLEO	MOTEL
TESICSAU	SUITCASE
CVOAINTA	VACATION

UNSCRAMBLE
ANSWERS 3

HAND DRAWN MAZE ANSWERS

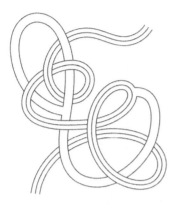

Solution 1

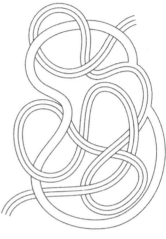

Solution 2

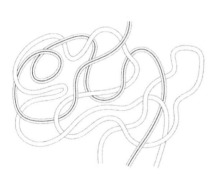

Solution 3

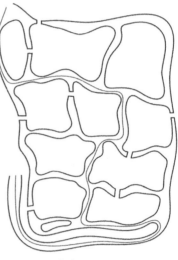

Solution 4

Solution 5

Solution 6

Solution 7

Solution 8

MAGIC SQUARE ANSWERS

ADD UP TO 15

2	7	6
9	5	1
4	3	8

ADD UP TO 65

9	3	22	16	15
2	21	20	14	8
25	19	13	7	1
18	12	6	5	24
11	10	4	23	17

SYMBOL MATHS ANSWERS

ANSWER 1

1	2	8

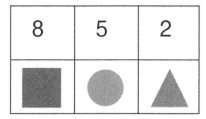

ANSWER 2

11	7	4

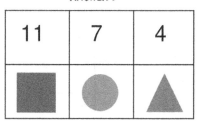

ANSWER 3

12	10	8

ANSWER 4

9	3	1

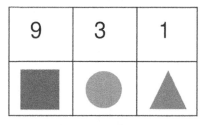

ANSWER 5

8	5	2

SUDOKU ANSWERS

Puzzle #1

6	3	2	5	1	4
4	1	5	6	2	3
1	6	4	2	3	5
2	5	3	1	4	6
3	2	6	4	5	1
5	4	1	3	6	2

Puzzle #2

3	1	6	2	4	5
4	2	5	1	6	3
2	6	3	5	1	4
1	5	4	6	3	2
6	4	2	3	5	1
5	3	1	4	2	6

Puzzle #3

4	2	6	5	1	3
3	1	5	4	6	2
5	3	4	1	2	6
2	6	1	3	4	5
6	4	3	2	5	1
1	5	2	6	3	4

Puzzle #4

1	6	4	2	3	5
3	2	5	4	6	1
4	3	6	5	1	2
2	5	1	3	4	6
5	1	3	6	2	4
6	4	2	1	5	3

Puzzle #5

3	4	1	5	6	2
2	5	6	4	3	1
1	3	2	6	5	4
4	6	5	2	1	3
6	1	4	3	2	5
5	2	3	1	4	6

SHAPED MAZE ANSWERS

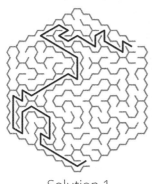

Solution 1

Solution 2

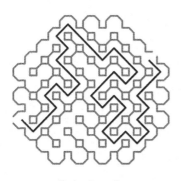

Solution 3

Solution 4

Solution 5

Solution 6

Solution 7

WILD ANIMAL CROSSWORD
ANSWERS

Crossword grid answers:
- 1. GIRRAFE
- 2. HIPPOPOTAMUS
- 3. LION
- 4. OSTRICH
- 5. HEDGEHOG
- 6. ZEBRA

Across
1.
3.
4.
6.

Down
2.
5.

ROAD TRIP
ANSWERS

Crossword grid answers include: FUN, DROVE, BRING, GAS, AW, WHEN, WHERE, CITY, TRIP, PAIM, CAR, RIM, MAP, ROAD, VAN, YET, PACK, P

DOWN
1. enjoyable
2. past tense of drive
4. a car needs this to run
5. not at home
6. past tense of go
8. a vehicle that has four wheels and an engine
9. when you travel somewhere quickly, you can say that you "made good _____"
11. to leave a car in a particular place
12. a vehicle that is larger than a car
13. a picture showing the roads of an area

ACROSS
3. take something with you
7. "_____ are we going?"
8. a place where people live that is larger than a town
10. a journey to a place
14. a hard flat surface for vehicles to travel on
15. Kids often ask: "Are we there _____?"
16. to put things into a bag to take with you

MATCHING FUN

ANSWERS

GAME 1

GAME 2

WORD FILL IN ANSWERS

Game 1

s	a	m	e	
		a		o
s	k	y	e	d
i				e
p	o	t		s

Game 2

t	h	y	m	u	s
			i		o
	w		x		l
c	o	d	e	d	
	k		s		
a	s	h			

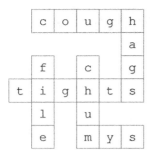

skyed
may
same
odes
sip
pot

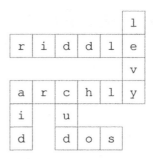

coded
woks
mixes
ash
thymus
sol

Game 3

c	o	u	g	h
				a
f		c		g
t	i	g	h	t	s
l		u		
e		m	y	s

Game 4

					l
r	i	d	d	l	e
					v
a	r	c	h	l	y
i		u			
d		d	o	s	

tights
hags
cough
file
chum
mys

archly
levy
riddle
cud
dos
aid

Game 5

```
n  t  h
   a     r  o  e
   i     o
s  l  o  w  s
   s     e
         d  u  h
```

Game 6

```
                  b
a  l  i  b  i
                  r
s  o  b  b  e  d
i        i
r        g  a  r  b
```

slows   sobbed
rowed   bird
tails   alibi
nth   big
duh   sir
roe   garb

HAMBURGER 21 VS FRIES 19

WORD SEARCH ANSWERS

Puzzle # 1

R	E	A	R	T	H		
Y	S	A	E	C	R	U	
D	E	E	P	T	I	N	Y
N	I	K	L	R	I	A	F
M	A	G	I	L	E	M	
	I	Y	Z	Z	U	F	E
	A	D	A	P	T	D	
			B	R	A	S	H

Puzzle # 2

	H	Y	P	P	A	H	J
D	U	S	T	Y			U
	S		A	M	C		I
D	E	V	O	L	R	I	C
N	D	L	I	H	C	I	Y
E	A	B	E	I	G	E	F
W	N		Y	G	G	O	F
B	I	R	C	M	I	L	E

Puzzle # 3

E	C	A	T	E	R		
N	U	A	S	I	A		
	U	L	L	U	H	U	E
F		F	B	M	R		F
U		L	O	O	C	C	R
N	F	O	R	M	L		E
N	D	O	T	E		D	S
Y			C	O	Z	Y	H

Puzzle # 4

T	O	T	R	E	L	A	
		O	D	M	A	R	S
M	S	Y	F	L	A	S	H
B	A	S	C	H	I	L	D
E	L	E	F	L	U	U	
I	T	A	R	I	O	E	B
G	Y		R	C	R	U	
E	N	A	G	E	V	M	D

Puzzle # 5

	C	J	E	V	I	R	D
	O	A	S	H	Y		
F	E	C	L	M	D		
L		V	A	O	M	I	
O	F	A	I	R	R	Y	K
W			B	L	E	N	D
D	I	R	T	Y	A		
		D	E	C	I	D	

Puzzle # 6

	E	T	D	N			
	R	Z	R	L	A		
E		O	A	E	O	L	
B	V	L	L	L	L	B	C
B	I	I	O	O	B	A	A
A	J	R	L	O	C	K	M
R	O		C	A	R	E	E
E	Y	C	H	I	L	D	L

Puzzle # 7

S		H	C	R	A	M	F
	S		R	U		I	A
	A	I	B	A	R	L	D
D	E	I	K	L	E	E	E
I	E	P	S	B	O	L	D
R	N	P	U	A	E	N	C
T		A	T	O		E	D
Y			W	H	C		W

MATCH THE ICONS ANSWERS

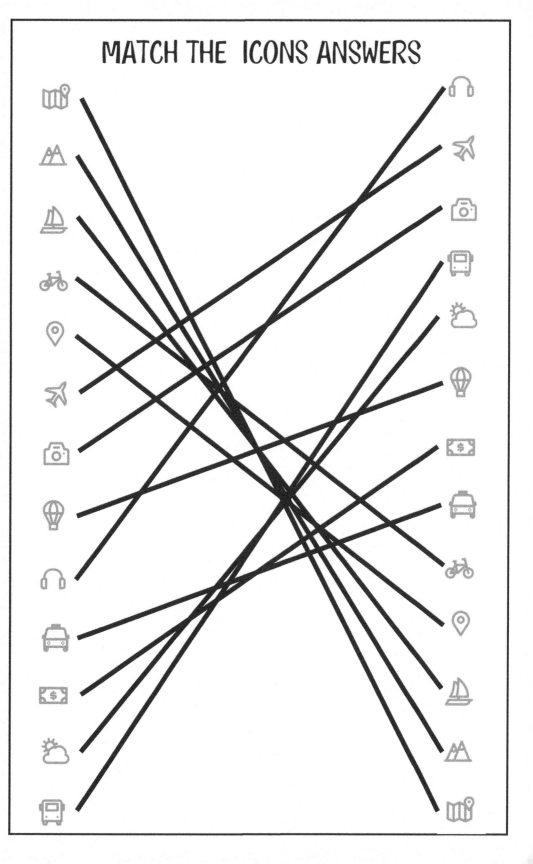

Made in the USA
Middletown, DE
19 July 2023

35455859R00051